Cover image © 1978 Bob Willoughby/mptvimages.com.

Cover design by Alan Coon Design
Layout by Fence Books

Published in the United States by Fence Books, Science Library 320, University at Albany, 1400 Washington Avenue, Albany, NY 12222, www.fenceportal.org

Fence Books is a project of Fence Magazine, Incorporated, which is funded in part by support from the New York State Council on the Arts and the National Endowment for the Arts, along with the generous sponsorship of the New York State Writers Institute and the University at Albany. Many thanks to these friends and to all Friends of Fence.

Fence Books are distributed by Consortium Book Sales & Distribution (cbsd.com) and printed in Canada by The Prolific Group (www.prolific.ca).

Library of Congress Cataloguing in Publication Data
Holiday, Harmony [1982–]
Negro League Baseball/ Harmony Holiday

Library of Congress Control Number: 2011923262

ISBN 13: 978-1-934200-42-1

FIRST EDITION
10 9 8 7 6 5 4 3 2

NEGRO LEAGUE BASEBALL

NEGRO LEAGUE BASEBALL

HARMONY HOLIDAY

THE 2011 MOTHERWELL PRIZE

ALBANY NEW YORK

FENCE
BOOKS

CONTENTS

I

II

V

Dwell like a ghost, black angel, dwell like a ghost.

—Doug Carn, *Spirit of the New Land*

I

A Rumor About More Earth

Dumbed fire of a carved pumpkin, starting the threshold of a Virginia porch, you look stepping, you look the pleasure feet burgundy, outstretched triply searching for girlhood and world and wood—you aren't my father

Hunched father in a harvest lantern starting the threshold of an antique porch, you too, stepping, looking the pleasure feet burgundy outstretched waltzing, searching for soft wood, unfurl, and good, you are my Fire.

My Thoughts on Fire

To give the best possible effect to a favorite object   Because we cannot help it, an anti-leveling
principal evokes a sanitary temperature called burn, and with it a color called crime and a texture:shine and
a swimmer: saint and a wielding air   and a dancer: remembered breeze and an end: in and an end (in),
andanending: never which is a form of revenge, and so the entire substance, which mistakes itself for
selfless, is only the keenest motion for resisting change: to become its champion, to summons it, a rigged
allure we cannot help opens itself to source and finds a father where the fire shorted, his build enormous as
all the houses swung out like an urge to drink rum right from the triangle   And so a gulf the opposite of soul
wedges between the human and his indication and becomes my empathy, for, neither can I, suggest myself
without destroying its most pleasurable aspect: oblivion and its havoc: someone else, and I love him: you,
caught in an escape : myself, and afraid to make an element make lament jocund The tenuous scent of
one lit on purpose is different than that of one that senses some superfluous earth then,   hurry up and light.

The Soonest People

I didn't see Jimmy's funeral

Jimmy's my father.

I missed my dad's funeral

Jimmy's my dad.

I didn't see the was coming

My father was Jimmy, dad

was weeping so frankly it came like gazing had

Two Tiered Alliance

Hey Dreamer   smile   like you're happy your mom got married   wearing that cascade on her head that says forever   so

Euphoric you nudge me and don't even notice, like the first time   you'd ever seen Moonwalk, Michael Jackson in glossed leather lured by zippers gliding

On a glide-built-aisle   down those eyes that hold like masts   and it'd be slick   to be a crisis scripted like brightmoments in that

we all know   there will never be peace   the notion of domain repeats around itself until there are no seats left in a stadium

Fuck Rome

The notion of plain repeats until there are no feet left without sneakers   that's a coma, not a dream   just a regular hardship case

Selling junk motors shined with waffle grease   to patient families who love the word

Sedan   suddenly   that ring of my mother's loving is a black eye   vision yielded to blood since the eye is
already a wound

from the beginning flung into looking   on the freeway, in a wedding dress made of favors and birth
Hey Runner, run like you're never

gonna be her   wearing that black gaze on your step wait stop   at the store for beer and candy, sandwiches
it's a celebration

no one change

Gone by Then

Gone then risen

Milk dawn gone then risen

Our ephemeral fawning done

Gone sanguine then risen in spell

High with your wrist while nihil busy

Unburrowing dice teams from sand figurines

Risen to swirl steam scooping passing seemingly

A kindred-ided up and up, born of dormant corners

Forms filial then filled   Goes mourn and swoon

Love have and love loom   Union and risen

ASSEMBLY

Every battery lined up like domino and grew the contrast of motor and nowhere as they buried themselves in each other's motion recklessness became a dance and a dance became every battery lined up like ready

Suspense is a kind of time, system of telling space from itself and the confession creates a sense of belonging   somewhere extensive, specific   no wrong, can do no wrong: homeland   Nor is my house a house nor is myself a self in the way they mean one occupant of one place called a body

It refrains

Every battery lined up in a station as the police check for accidents, no my mother hadn't slipped when she had fallen that maximum down   there is a constant effort, we feel it   as agency   one commits to behaving in a certain way and ceases to motor, matter, my mother, with her casual sense of a language of the household scaffolded by words for average moments by words for disaster, for happier, bywords, I can't think of any now but maybe purified by the effort hiding its failure watch her slump into the one rubber chair until she amuses with the automatic of her own sacrifice or fact or Edith Piaf or *As You Like It*, the right clothes, the right desperation looks indignant and I am dizzy backwards each time I laugh about while I cry for her, demiurgic as our mild sorrow it runs, bang! into ecstasy.

Death by *Then*

Charred septic except I'm thinking the color green, a thawing of it, warmth like I'm thinking three shades yawning to clear the silence in my ears have never appreciated… but You-Sound-Kin. A wizening, a new shrewd issuing sing, for him. I'm listening green, not like splendor, like latitude, for you a cleft gruesomeness treading itself scentless poppies seeping us noxious, my favorite hue and the context you care in, the color you carry the color, cousin the color, cousin and color, for lust towards husk sounds, carboned around the paranoia of ignoring a lover and a mother and a sister as inert glimmers of family grow vulgar or oliver, vinegar green, I'm thinking of two passings growing back, growing one verde arrogate, thinking it irritates me to pursue a canyoned longing to rural green renewal, drawl green, Iowa wasn't green, shag carpet green, still thinking the grass which grows out of tar shoulder, the carved shrug toward our such slick road. I'm last green of an August funeral, struggling to depict what's kept thinking.

Then, the tempo you move me to, an indignant softness, an agnostic softness, not sure I aperture the way I want it, gaunt island to peninsula neck green, soma muscle buking. I'm mummied map of the family album where your gauze is August sun vapor on sparrow wing pavement, mother blooming through cracked pattern, all greens burn. Then, a cistern of earned desire, a missing, a choir of chapped feet to dry earth rejoicing by then.

Hens

If you bring up orange juice and a farm to a June month, there will be no more hunting and we can understand our lungs again. If I come to love you but don't believe in conclusions, there you will be again, if you dial the battle until we run out of revolutions, still the matted ribbon bend coloring air with one nerve, still the tough inertia of power, shortens when you talk about seeds, Booker T. Washington, whose name is so jawed it clicks. I adjust to the accentuations when you undo them, money, money, money, money, one two, one two, and yen

Then, the way you breath up the ribbon tension, an envy to say short of speaking, tape recorder telling me the mercenaries have spouses, the hard gray pants, antsy ramble of silt beneath dress shoes, emphasis distilled and then amplified, if you bring up walking this means preamble, part Cherokee part Mephistopheles if you bring the police who chant our boundaries' embellish, it is for their uniforms that you look so fresh with that ground in your hands and that phantasmagoric endlessness

HOME NEGATIONS

Though, evenly, to the face of the cage, as an expatriate convinced past place is past. Put past. The idea of place. The task of Isis, demon, cactus.

—

And the fact of infatuation and of space means to him-and-there, one same affinity to the contour of commerce, comes assimilated for affection—call them areas and brothers. So I affect a love for what I live on, as in, they love the shapes of tenements and levees and alleys and seedless fruit sizes, and build a bias around them, trigger by receiver, by tunnel shins.

—

But he knows what to investigate without the stigma of build-up.

He loves such as this knowing, soberly and buckled

He sobers such with this loving of he-knows-what building

Thing I call a structure, hinge, of course, is his brother area, offer, calling, Georgia aired

—

Not to recite the psyche for the recent but to court them in concert

Not to want what they know, but to have the nerve to want it or not
the nerve but the bravery of shape   to take place   which is to contradict affection similes

You feel like my country, my state, my ecclesial sake, sake as you are my situation

my phone gun   my celebration atom Ma-at my caught up   my rule my royal and other than him are just
opinions   un-uglying the 'as', in

When you walk, sad road across your own movement, what doesn't diminish is the distance between
states of belonging, which is infinite along your color, your pace, your hand one harp in the air and one in
the stomach. And when, up the intuition of noise to fill itself parallel, you speak of them as just travel, just a
visit gait and impasse, phase of aloof in your hovered dactyl against this news outstretch—a tipped parade
farewell to the loosest heritage

LIKE I'M SIMPLE

Still. The word *pursuance* turning nuance to itself, then us. Still. Either end of a reinvented action acts history (as) so what does this mean, to be centering ongoing/during/now means forgetting or stealing inertia from a

                          laughter is permanently in a middle, and why can't his haunt me, in fact, I forget how it sounds, and the muting image of his disengaged mouthing haunts easier: psalm Read any and still feel abridged, healed, ubiquitous   the endemic serenity of a grand lie is truism by restlessness   proof of forever, still   true that it is my thumb invisible ovaling his lips that blocks an outburst of impersonations of laughing-out-loud in a cave, out a fence

The madness of great men occurring to themselves as vigorous noise

Still (so that I have to think of my father) to continue or unless I prefer to hear you assimilating your sensibility to anybody's, telling-clean-joke   like you're a phony, still. So that I have to   you request hot grits and a loose piano slammed down on by a kid hand Accidents are also requested by lovers too coward and children too ignored   still   on purpose   so that I have to move

Like I'm symbol   so that I have become competitive with my history which I place in a laughing cave   or in a practical disaster like   h o m e   still   no more moving

Ideas are the saddest thing   Ideals are the next saddest

II

MAN AT HOME

It's probably dark there but the scarcity deep in your voice Whiskey shoe shine boy brother boy, sir, is nearly a hurt I can handle and maneuver,   "Good Love" and the Al Green verse for severance as gone, lay your head on and on the empty room swept for the scent of breath with a phone in the hand left glass in the next, room, another no one can hear the plumbing underneath and how to keep dignity from crime, shiny crime weaned restless with these creaking pipe and oaks,   and which hand screws the pick to its I-am-a-Black-Panther speechless affirmation, trick ego turn the fucking page in that Penthouse Afraid to go back to Alabama from LA, and they call you a case of anxiety weaned of arrivals, an approach to hiding and arrival, and they crook keep   You are also just used to the seethe of privacy vice deed be cool man, be cool man we know that   we know that badly.

A Child's F.Y.I.

Alleys are made of stages. Objects that you can get on and enter and compass. Spectators whistle with all their might, I close with all my might-could.

Halos are made of narrow, foam, glare, the aroma you expect when you walk into love, or fall is all quiver aloud, all laws out.

I am proud of the things I favor, so sore from them. African's Heals, real move, malarkey, copper, lucre off proof, burr green and bergamot, polyester until I look like a jazz trumpeter's best wife. Eager, and the way my sister, no matter how many strings and sir-men, learned the word trifling backwards and heard it lift

CHOREOGRAPHY TO EITHER

The crossing guard and my sister

He says she has small eyes and her spunk is resultant

She launches a tumultuous resistance / she stands still in the middle of his streetpost until she is *holding* still with the will of a millennium

Together, these take to swaying, a dazed cabaret, and then (sudden-chested) exhibit separate inklings that happen to match as they separate, afraid to match. A cavern bat encouraging air where there is shelter matter, by leaving towards it, splits death with misconception, with his magnet, adjunct (blank) from its own drag—Attachment

Where there is nothing left to admit, I picture the traffic, her in its urges, peripheral and dagger, a union captain with his hat, halving arms as a fascist would, navy nylons like the ones I'll strap on, some hydrogen blond from the beauty shop, from can't see in the morning 'till can't see at night, the nimblest sheets of silk with no pills, white by way of silver, killjoy grabbing color from until, there is one thing left to admit, I wave at it by instrument fingers and save the palm pulling her into view, plastic, and sufficient kitwood and scramble for dew as if it would settle our good water.

Walking off the offer to where   *I stay clean just looking clean*

CRISSCROSSING IN THE DARK

Intelligence is about pain and unteaching. When I forget about you I feel smarter, but when I can ignore the pain I feel naive and tame doom. A passage about war. A pact to not war. A pact toward a path about in *Clockwork Orange* when they watch the film within the film with their arms helmed into a rest. Helmed is a journalism, not even a radio show. Unrest is about intelligence and for what reason do my muscles remember to cross my legs when my mind knows this stagnates the blood. Is my blood a brain running solid unto plasma swallowed by its own intelligence/cells when they restless tell us, tumor, tell us, certainly dying is the source of over-living, ever-living. Tell us, slow wind with the Orange Moon song, slow down, close sel(f) around. Life is in the corner of my blood stuck, at the kneecap needing as a lady to have a habit which breaches her health, I chose this and my family is about the street in Mississippi made with three-wheeled buggies and cousins and maybe an aqueduct and crowded with all this empty which is the acoustic soon, I think of you again and feel assent and infinity and the sweet what-for of a vertical jump on my Bribing Trampoline, consecutive knees hexagon around a compass which points to none of us is eager enough, numb enough, junked enough to think such a thing, to think sucker thing, so superstitious for transparency that we start tilting it toward its own disking.

Preemptive

You can raid my escapes, while I await yours hostage, bated, digital eight shaped, a patient assembly of tottering body, neotony, growing out my knees into now's sheepish chic privacy ecstatic with the personality of speechless.

DUETS

Coldlaugh, lowfire. kin, imagined. Cannonball Adderly, Banyon tree, makes-me-see-you-again. We do so and the season grooves to no close.

Pulsewire and Pulsefloat. The night is supposed to float right bold, right because of you, and your elders and your slow delve tells me Leadbelly sells his speed well. Beads fly off of sinewire, pearls maybe, vibrate away from the rich wrist and make tell on magic. Snickering, waterbacked, she has many others and drinks to this earth's affluence.

Hot laugh, burn badge, dandy laughing grabs his teeth from shimmeeman, Bojangles or Pin-up. Keep smiling, we do, in Soweto, in the wildelm, in the highrise, in low car, live, and the season times our speech, too quickly, too many words reaching one another, said.

Sinking pulse and rope beat. Hiatus is a needle, somebody dull be trusted. Just don't suck your teeth, just keep your mouth neat and stutter enough convincedly. Suck your teeth, just don't stutter each over horror, bad for life force, ash, your fascination muscle. Finish the upheaval, bow, heal. Just don't leave the table looking as tidy as display would. Should you feel displaced make everywhere messy, massive, good as you have it.

Rolling pulse and laugh opening, the folklore for capture source. Saxophone around soaking bounty. Black town around black country. Back country, continent, *Tensity* by Cannonball Adderley, Rensetso holding a piece of oak out to spoken language, we go as the season sends its crows as cuddlewind, muttering there's-a-size-for-him, there's a seize for him, theirs is a city in full season

Opium pulse, Gil Scott Heron. Chromeclose. My hero, my heroine, never mind my looking in to the anytime restaurant to the dialed eyes, never mind the personal child at the diner table, pulse groomed to fold over like cornsilk at the bottom of a celibate hill, folding his hands until they blotch and strangle and land

in the conversation.

Empire, so lonely. Bent pulse, stuck laughing. We won't be, maybe, mad so much as relieved, to talk fast again, around the fire fence, by then, land names, campaigns for silence. The brightest day I can remember since love was earning it. Pittly pulse went to fist pulse, child at the table reading lips and speaking the difference. My foot sleeps, bygones, kind beat, the kind we're mindless keeping, look behind you, stood behind you. I have no time to say the kind of pace I reach to know you, no quickquickslow, new, soak poppy seeds in barley to check for birth, knew to check for rebirth, knew to stop between maneuvers, to be nervous for glory, to show people as they see themselves is another thing like   mothering.   I would be marching, I would be leaping and jury, and seed money, you would smell the tease without covet. Each pulse struggling to release the other, we make an archive or tumble parts of starved blood, the fullest laughter two bodies can muster ours record and do, playing spoken for each other.

LONELY VESSEL

Berlin in a crank, say *d a r l i n g*. Berlin/darling. Nearly mean anger for the letters infringing upon their anchors to mint up statues who cool us carve for carve. Mandingo in Berlin and Josephine and the gallivant and the Jesus Sandal and the disgruntled yellow man, omnibus, strolling bliss onto his disposition guts grumbling on some spacious hunger of passengers fecund from lurking   Germany was everybody's word for forward, in Berlin everywhere.

For him I am Italian and for cache African and for the black American and foregone capital, all hollow gravity art/sing, darling, I can float on a raft sink that city, and rickshaw in one piece—inevitable renewal, you look a stoic glamorous, tossing your stammers in your hips, it's sharp, your charm hinge on your gimme, gimme, chest in your arms, jumping, like a famous junkie

Newcomer and Obedience

I bud, more at look... I, oculus, occult, double bye, goodbye again, departure coded of hint, to speak about the heart along mind rhythm, carve, jealous of the whole car and other partially intimate machines   Dim try to introduce an organism into an organism: vaccine, cave, instant place   Binoculars on a saddle, sad close, a crash: but not the one we're in, which is blatant as child love as asked in, cove, oven, chimney, pleased, and the mother again, looking out the window of a bias as penguins at the doorstep police it with their cold shift: she says, don't let him in, so I don't let him in.

Then suppose he could hear me that noon dream, strapping his militia vest and turning pirouettes in the mirror, because it made a dress on me and something special fancy about the dead metal left to funeral in the fabric and something still answering from the babble dialogue of these scenes is a courtship a fit of irony awaiting its bias   The way we live the child again and again, against the love, against the memory is why

Certain Ballads

It's said that he resisted and they beat him with sticks   in the first report for Pilgrim   he claims to be a musician, claims to be in a Broadway band   trading choruses, playing chorus for chorus, as in a streetfight, so jealous wage your experts   so they sent him to Creedmore, a New York facility   for electro convulsive therapy   Mercury and crickets have my mind in common, he'd explain   on the piano bench coordinating hallucinations into Dartaniun   A manifestation of cycling time

She had hid his shoes, to keep him from leaving saying *He is in a state of grace, he practically asked me to do it, actually*, but she had too many adverbs, too many qualified actions, indicating too many urgings, and asunder   How we were staggering together through the streets where they keep flags and yachts until the morning watched us lean indoors, a terrible ordinary day   How we were staggering through the streets together between flags and yachts, forming calluses we wouldn't even notice on the bottoms of our empty footage   how bearable you've made it, beyond my wildest motives

III

Nine Key Chord

Or nothing is really north, but you're so civic and indivisible.

The Folk Revival has no middle, no anachronism, just no more caption or advent, but you're not them dilettantes.   As relentless as listening to the shore backwards, your words about how it happens, wanderlust and continental, badge verse the nourish of no mercy crash short, burst slack,   repeat as you were *reallysomething*.

You know the house is empty, exempt, yours for the mentioning of will to power appears an officer on a horse with more posture than you're used to, undoing your robe for it's satin loose before a sash and give him the magician, night minion, answer over the flashlight   *nothing*

Authority I admire is kept during itself, kinetic, black market uncorrectable and in between admiring and participating, you wear the tight number which hugs risen the been-there under your eyes vindicates evasion head on   I don't even imagine what real violation sounds   I stay at the Social Club while you go sell my high back to Cuba China   as a kind of sound of king of sound   He'll ask me to speak up, come closer, note the kind of trouble I'm in here is absurd and prolific   the kind you catch for witnessing an author rewrite the book   skip the vista, the word vista, the good word   and look as it's splitting

HIM AT HOME

He drowns in a mountain lake I am on the brink of crossing

INDUSTRY

A gunshot then. Stop your bikes and let them wobble in mechanism

Then a gun watchman, hithered on the imaginary end of a macabre

lipping telescope, broke my hero into speeches.

It had to be masculine this many occasions consecutively and also diminutive from a hugeness I could not collect enough pipes and wizards on the trumpet trigger to build a trumpet or remorse or capitulate or boost my chest into order, for a basicness distortion gives, gives exegesis   Pedals coiling and scuffing the earth dust trusting lungs to come out in funicular or jigback. If I could just look to the minimalists, suss a sleek black wrist gathering the handles or clutching stacks of hourglass glasses to his grappling ribs at this one endless shop.   We looted

An Assassination from Appropriation Forms

Pocket crops the Mississippi Delta into the shifted gloss of a Polaroid. Devendra hoist sits on his loyal show beads, juxtaposing fists with dice, like you've ever been there besides to pick up material and rare

that Jimmy finishes wearing his hat down that babbling lane you call a district a settlement

a treason to keep tame

                                        canceling the aesthetic of when

he drops it and runs after mirage, fix

PCP aggressive

got god wind of family in the French Quarter got, je suis into Jesuit, his I am from this picture neon with teeth and fib, Mississippi tumblelived   hilless on the numb food number three, food Tuesday

Rational numbers from a nuclear assembly-and-a-half they half daddy   pocketing the culinary heat of finity as captaining   He is keeping a child for his Stetson and begins to step lithe over the pick-up, a rival sense of sabotage   a docile home daughter who watches him shadowbox like she's coaching a champion or Moses

And then hymn steps in the from of him, *lend me your teeth, lemme your teeth*, and he's done shooting him before he knew how to die.

Negro League

Overcome with testimony is one way   home (run), is another way to blame   only another name for one type of company   creaking porches   kool-aid pitchers, typical laughter applied over a lack and through a metal bat hitting a hollow ball king (all) up into either base you choose   a new game   call it/calls out   lips stained with cane and red number color of poor thing or pouring   looks so rich though in the diamond lit up championship bleachers   One town entirely intoxicated, surfaced by the play of its own story into a more reasonable tradition

Assured that it will get better and that it is will and that the willow is a pale notion of this type of unshapable pain is a form of ability and inevitable and made more so by the fact that it pledges into a community's every drinking and winning and porcelain and the sullen hint of light in the corner of the absence in your eyes   Is that remorse or prize for

places to be

We need places to be.

God, style, I live there sometimes (as in, I am occupied) with the other oppressed and decadent women-is-the-nigger-of-the

-world clenched in the act of identity formation, but I believe in it more than your stuffy Midwestern palm, more than your stuffy New England palm, more than the high five pink ping of oncoming night, more than nightly, hourly, more than brown rice or any other plagiarized pasteurized stable pastor

        my legs shut into echo chambers scuffing themselves for, that is no way to live, the way god did, jesus   vindictive orphan document sense of sustenance other than   *What a dumb-what dumb-whatitidone*, to deserve so much tilt until I can see your every receding as if it is building itself into me, from me   And we compensate

I mean we make a baby

I mean we horde capes

I mean restored and vagrant

I mean no more Baseball, Football,

Allegory of the Cave or Plato,

or behavior or sweet or home,

savior, no more punishment for anything

but nowhere

I mean we say we mean it

because it feels nice to mean

anything—it feels childlike a newborn

lost in a beautiful cave on the way to

behavior—it feels and fields and home

and safe only saved, like a packet of foreign sugar

back pocket cafe good nigger swagger—wait.

I went ahead, became teenager, sure

and important careers became owners of purchasers

of property   I mean it means something, you know what

and no telling

I mean when we say something out loud

or play something outside

　horseshoes or

pi as 3….. I, or just catch, Sore palm, yours

makes me happy

as I don't know why

Biography

Armistice and a sudden, all of my dresses are new again (a new cast or I'm fresh orphan) Tension is of this kind of whistle you call a lilting (hen-shrill, means) solipsism when you called: hill, an alternative to climbing itself hill/he'll you calling telegram for every minor worn in man of and fellow man of and sell out man of and husband and detail oriented bill paying citizen man of sequins from the '40s style one worn to court, man of new proportions of man of again man of call me a warrior or corridor man of rise, though, man! you are falling and not a dream

Skylark and other standards deform with a changing perception of width and downstep and (in) don't step superstitions about motherhood being lethal or controlled by its own production or (folk) product, not a good, god, (being) a service god news anchor flashes bleached teeth and press on lashes god hill he'll (the way I want to say) one word out of its haunt is backwards when I call your name specifically into walking (transit)

A/way to paint a sculpture as to give up art for art- (why would we want to/color you) man you so suffering the beautiful things have grown perverse in their transfer from hang to glimmer in your eye.... kind of don't care how he'll tell the story uphill, a jesus (gasp) a couple of jazz

Absolutely

Maybe we're the media.   Burial   feet   a junk Adam. Adjuncts from some hunger done of ambidextrous visions   This one was just glancing at the vinepiece, mise-en-scène, beat machine, the same person jumping land into building—an electronic volume, tight jeans wearing-thinking maybe we're the animal, brand new scape immediately translated into dub from debut into

Objectively rooted, the support develops, people go where people go, traveling in teams and stories, maybe we're a medium, curtaincannon breathing bigger for critical amounts of us want to be, recently, gone through, or going through, traversed   Little finally numbers upheavaled about before or defunct shrill rushes of integrity alleviated by pocket calling pocket ring, *hello*.

—

He has held me in the middle, rowboat, rowboat, wave, the entertainment, at least we are the entertainment, and instructions for how to use ourselves or install our uses, watch me wash me no standing no blank keep anytime keen enough to act minor and all, *you dig*, accurate and also wrong

(by the time you ask, the bashful archeologist is a black and blushes and furiously but the blush cannot be seen or determined)   like an absolute   Tycoon to be mellow tune to your   *This is a disaster how we pay them, to watch us* Mafia unto Mafia I've set my seek above

ALLTIME

And every time I fall in love, what television, another obituary, I am three, trying to tell psychology about psychology: look at me, see me, watch me.

One Single Thing

You're courage, your ridges, your moments of protection. Your tenacious, you're hypocrite, you're not going to let on. I watch you wield. It's appalling. My swallow heavies, abiding silver, even as it takes me to its color, makes me lack yours. It's lingering towards something, then retracting, then collapsing hackneyed into its units, today and today-to-today to today, infinitives elate from their progression, and can quench themselves without swallowing wokeness.

You meant to be so slick that you couldn't even look at anyone. The money leaves this corner, parlor, worn in part of hard for the dealership, the card game the cliché, the shake. I can't make you boil yams, take sand paper to the stubborn made, ask for acres instead of shake. Your convulsions, your vulpine, your timing is loaded. I steal memories from myself, to leave you in them and sheltered. Back and forth are tired, sensibility is tired, henchmen are tired, a pension for strikes airs itself as your likelihood to be there, in your resonance, your beckon, your snare, your timbre's a burlesque pinned down.

We're lucky for lack of deities, we're lucky to pass idols and mistake them for sale, we're lucky one pale holds things and another's electing blood, we're lucky we ate that dirt in Iowa, we're lucky haiku unbuckles, lucky shuttling's the feeling and not shut, we're lucky the lady means to be a healer, we're lucky for trots for word for word, and this field's higher weather for earth or not.

VISION STATEMENT about the name Menelik

Late in the nighttime I see banisters on certain androgynous hats and ask them indoors, removed or distorted and what kind of accident is a sudden puppet or a luck that tugs at its own tradition, pretty dancer?   Feedback loop of fortune, not a wheel for such linear horizons, stock, bonds, steering, quiz shows: pretty dancers   All examples of why I want to learn to walk on stilts (I am better at being partial around machines and high things, mothers dancing) also

Muhammad Ali   if we're talking about/some pretty dancer

Down Beat with Betty Carter on the cover, if we're gonna discuss a pretty dancer

Stella, a pretty dancer

Menelik, most pretty dancer

not-a-care-pretty-dancer

in the Whole Wide World Announcer

says:

the Gospel is not primarily that at all, pretty champion

Prince, conqueror, pretty dancer

buggy, pretty dancer

university university university

put me to sleep

I was gone   a solitary octopus/ pretty dandy

I didn't wear any long purple or long

  any more

moves

didn't I dance for you, pretty gladhand me something

weren't we something,

a chief would be   We find out he was a chief so we imagine feathers on jet jet heads, propellers

and command, we imagine a man saying: get over there be a community

and threatening to prove the possibility singlehandedly, by joining himself, city killer

he looks of a silicone lonely in

asynchrony about the *Jet* magazine with Ornette Coleman on the cover

saxhanded, going to show

he does not look sluggish there but the logo does—lovely thinking

to us, for us   thinking dancers   and pretty thinkers   saluting an intuitive delusion   that we're in, so we're in

IV

VISITING ENGLAND/ A MANIC HONOR

If there is a blue horse, I'm here to say there's a blue horse

If you are my mother, they're going to say, you took good care

If they are going to say, they are part of gone anyways—

there's your blue horse   And you hand me a wad of money

and Kleenex right out-of-pocket, so I spend and weep at the invisibility of each comparison,

I have some new things

Warriors running the London marathon need a well where they're from, horse is a new animal

blue is a new eye, London is a two drum

Europe offers a new way to be concerned, to be concerned is a new shape for grief, for griefshape—
your sponsorship and infinity

High Concept

I. That Conversation

Raisins and smiles for me and my sisters/

Your beauty arranges me into sheep, daddy   Warm Army

might be saying she is brat for wanting to watch him babble

when he might be saying t r a i n e d s o l d i e r or her name, aloud

Disobedience, so it repeated, cancelled flight like more important in its yield-like: fighter dogs

or the word p a u-ci-ty into be still with me   pause   daddy papa keep up, though,   you remind me of
my range   from frantic to susceptible   to now

II. Two ways...:

Sara went to Jail

I go in school

Debby is at the hospital, getting better

Mom is   what to say   living   getting better

Sara will be chef

Debby will be in shows   a girl in chose

mom will host us and know what (doctor, suspect)

I will let you know

Your beauty estranges the rest   and need is dangerously similar to expectation, except dignity   you know
I want more all of sudden, moral lumber, somewhere-I-have-only-traveled is where I want to live now

III. Proxy

The main reason why they beg is to learn humility   ripe incidents come into my knowledge as an affinity
to marvel, too stunning you are sunny hoodoo morning   a free word to mean   sublime meaningfulness
in a moment of disorder and shortage or dawning ashamed of its own balmy mysteriousness like the Mona
Lisa-you, light up in the abdomen, a whole city clamors crimson disturbance   longing for suffix, longingly
and the durability of a true love/cover, explained by the lure of any spell cooped up in its legacy of procedure,
exploited for executive-decoy, say, reading the Ovid over Mel Gibson action, triumph of a posture-hear
didn't you hear me   push is not reason to push, the main reason why they beg is to learn took from took-
from

He is too ready

He is pronouncing keen in two syllables

ke-en   ke-en   kee-n   kee'na ken-etic, connected, can't read it but slim key pressed F minorest
incredulity, none of the announcements' nonsense amount to the kind of warning I need against any more
dying

as a penalty of doing-by as a penultimate dignity as quiet as in between goodbyes   beautyisa-rarething
barrier to and bearing intuition   I think you are super   (I think of him first)

sent in earnest (I sent it)

I think you are perfect (he's alright, with me)

I think you are true (I know he can tell too)

I think you are pivot (turn around)

I think, how precarious a habit (it) is, to be impressed (remarks, not literature)
by the distance between us, which we both invented of (the never enough that there is—none of What's
happening is   as   the universe is   expanding

LETTER TO BY AND BY

Chances you are my Chances

Sweepstakes

Ever Since

They make it about how ever since the sweepstakes the yard is empty. Also, Maynard Ferguson versus his own accretion of inverse and how come ever since chances you've become my chances and they have, ever since the day out loud been steady called hologram expansive contest love made about an interim between carpent and hunter.

Also my sister's early Jezebel version of come home gets mentioned on some slogan and anywhere, an anywhere you play,

you play the record ever since territory, shall have meant the universe, made about yard and dowry readymade and south lipped. I pick the kind of power sullen never nullified by how-come-it's-yours, by and by.

To My Paloma, My Tough Dove

The things we know are Gigolos, locusts, hoax crushing up.

My sister, tough as corners, crushing up the things we know.

Are Gigolos locusts or just the stroke of it, whistlers and moguls?

The sisters we know are thrushing corners for Gigolos so

for corners, the things we know storm.

The things we know are rigged giddy, pornographic

The already things—jigjig, slow-slow.

My sister knows a Gigolo, called Daddy,

where did up go,

my religion of the things we know of

nothing like locusts

Sluts are nothing like locusts.

Us kids, us kids just learned to whistle.

The things we'd know were whistleblown, colloquial

My sister stuck in corners to support her daddy, man

born whistling, the things we know are open

hoaxing cut from shadows

my sister rose a Gigolo flat—

a kind of murder, a kind of payback for things we know

The parallax of throat habits, the rapture of switching death

with the shrill lack of custody

Dixie is a two beat thing/11:11

Yes I love the man with the double hands who crammed my head intop the basin, and when I lunged up for air said shotgun, went found the pick camouflaged on the piano and held it through me Yes I conjugate him as after but his name went like fast Jim and Jedward, a special graphite in your mouth as water crowded Yes and I love the way he runs   A number counting down coming down rubber rung hill eleven one too, one two quilted pigtails fell below shoulders all vestigial like I'll call him a fellow as it holds enough of a pillar of a formal illness distilled is this love,

11:11

(there is something comforting about the beak of one and the trunk of one and the tongues we speak in and some-junk-we-done)

There were four of the same thing rising, clean-mines, intending one side-side/by-side, and this was my trial/a problem/obnoxious

I love him

I love him

I love him

I love him

The box invents them insides, mentions viable/unbearable/tidiness, four half-roofed arrow, Eros, a pike in my groove—vote

invitation

invitation

blue trivia

maneuver

Children change the subject   exaggerated clap   changes, the object changes to a task-how graduation-how audience, how pandering bracket-cactus

watch them

watch them

watch-out how (they catch sense)—

looking

As if men as if booking agents, epidemic-rookies and sages and just as and just is an antiseptic critic in...
not-in-London quid pro quo fix—I want to get away

young/ make-believe/custody/a safe race

run in and run in and run in un-ruined

HOUSE TO HOUSE

Coin in me, put by you, falling

Pending the female sense that

I cost something and that that

is my identifiable worth

I pretend a slot for dowry

crimes and offerings.

Teen couples buy themselves

designer watches again

this Halloween, not to costume, not to

dress up but to mean time has come

rendered like a banded possession—matching, leanedin, ticking, ongoing music of next—

I jog through these places, neat paces of celebrate, odd cinema faced as actual, pastel gray sweat pants and a plastic neon swatch counts the miles secondhand daises rake the pulse for Sweetback   I like to feel chased, until I am being chased outofmyshoulders, off road, track, and lens aperture

After a walking stick smithereen (Penny rolling tar, the smallest, tannest, unit of wish United States has, newsprint in me, wrote by you   calling these investments, savings. Tells me I behave like a fund, an exponent, and how much fun it is to expect the difference to exceed origin and repeat

                Bottom, I do not believe in one   polished   vortex narrower at the core because I do not believe in anything yet or before or future except that displacement has been one revolution, meaning I turned around and said your name one time one syllable a bud one system and I've been collapsing from the heave of your invisible trust ever since, so money is an opinion where love an opinion we've worn into preference

dimelemon

dingy indian dollar

watermelon, tobacco, phonebooth, collard, gentleman caller,
glass, zoo glass as

heteronyms for near to you I am a woman some far away lady your gaze approaches

II.

Now you've come here with me at the nickel mashing the nickel into a sea shell microphone and we build a speech through the value and into intuitive use, clone a value attempting to prove ourselves of no reason but hungry which brings empty which brings the temptation to feed and to count again, we, now, and memory   These many languages I favor into one swoop of order: that I need to exempt water, to tension air, to land-land, terrain, when, there you are looking famous as a coin face, vague and exchangeable word for yourself, my any abolitionist, my gambling habit, I forget your name, but lights flash, and win pour out, and I use the loud metal for our house-place to go place, another round.

THE COME UP

Retreat is when he says *needles fencing* and I see the scent of poppies backing away from their opiate tense, future perfect. It's hard to be somebody's. Freeze tag. Allegedly I am sister somebody caught soft running, pretty little theme, helpless desire, automatic going after, a moving destination, raspy freight

And somehow I wish you were with this vantage, not pressing it, not scanning it for fix this time.

Shawnuf

An eagle, a fulcrum, an underneath. Someone will grin for me, and someone will winnow, someone will win me my dopamine and someone will win me clean. In the meantime, I put honey to your gun seams, the slow goes shooting, machines so proven breed

malfunctioning, and aloof and swinging—someone's will's flying, sutures and Clydelike   Lukewarm, I'm used to yours, to brutal, to sprawl-lunged, to gone some, one will limber will member will bend first, while the other serves ransom

Woman Home

This Diamond Noon, can you, room in me, recede room, pay the fee, the feed, beast up, and do it again these againagainagain people, me people, copious minded, believe I'm with my oath the,

                    road shaped belly loaded flagrant light of mineral,

though, don't propose to me on that extraction, but do please say something into halves and centrics.

My turn turn tricks, can you sense it—the fending of genes and sentiment and persona and the known of sowhat sense,

howcome sense,   redundant

convention's unkempt density against my gendered slow breath and revoke

Then again, timeand, can you have meant in me a clear piece of money, she wonders, turns over, closes the sheets and locates herself repeatedly spends herself on each occlusion

v

AMBASSADOR

He said some thing about Philadelphia clay

Bafflement and its quotient climate, apathy and its quotient climate

I asked   how could you make this city stepping out into a globe of itself imploding, tell me in your own words how to be more like you, love in a space of acute attention to limits: marionette streetlamp, sculpture of a landmark murmuring about art in the age of mechanical   hush

Wear house shoes to the market and grab your daughter's hand in traffic and catch her stacking rivers in yard dirt   merrily, my father, a front a sea a flood, a Marxist, I love you.

And so I knew to check for rebirth, knew to stop between pursuers, to be nervous at glory   To show people as they see themselves is still another thing like   other thing

Playing House

Lover with an advertising accent, all empty altitude and glove compartment narcotics, alligator is the new word for   hold on while I rummage nonsense for the registration, wait, I don't drive,   hold on while I learn how to admit my liabilities in the form of a diorama housing an upsidedown pyramid dangling from the sinew in a robot's middleback. Rib, my mother   coveted a stuffed monkey and had named him Zip in early Southside Chicago suburb, and I romanticize that that's where she's lived, child of Sicilian pub owner grandfather, chewer of vintage gum company veal, vermouth over a keeled gin. I was a kid afraid to swallow, throat constricted, videotape of *King Kong* in a coral along the larynx, and I could hear the evidence finally sinking, pulled string in my center, anterior, the forced gulp of impact of being seen that stuck (young to catch zebras fucking at the wild animal park and think they're choking, beg an adult to save them, pull 'em apart, fool in a park)—maybe just needs a push up the tucked up pyramid, while asking, will you gimme a boost, already   holding my air in order to swing the bars better, with trepidation's agility and a performer's false effortless. A mother wanted to become a singer, Zip was pitch noir, nappy, character for a factory face. He wore a shake which was a dishevel, and a hat, which jail, no outfit but primitive ribbon rags and the cherry dye numberever, a tongue, its uncouth set of visible nerves. Still that. One morning, more than one, wake your black ass up, my mother would enter laughing in the hind tone a meanness so used to itself that it keeps itself company, is bitterness and envy and birth and being born and regular.

The New Breed

The tragedy is not that it happens but that we do not accept it

  somebody says, Saturday and you believe he means that then will be miraculously revised from a huddle of disclosures to I most certainly will not notice your badass singer is high on crack   that diva   not just cause somebody says

     Nor will I keep mesmerized by pencil tracing hands, because it is erotic, it is remedial   A child goes to counseling for (this, practice) self-examination as his mother goes to listen   they are offended by each other's importance

and the very offense surprises them into that shy enmity between people too similar to accept one another Every weekend a sense of justice preserves the ethic (of disgust, trajectory, going back, catharsis, a system   somebody's square heart) a thick batter of egg, sugar   a sense of what next, shit is and what it will be   tenderness toward   resistance   to cool hunting   then back to the work which is paper tiger paper tiger rock tiger rock band card deck, denial   sharp side down just

Short of dying, being with him felt abortive   the loss of belox in the body, siege   daddy's corvette giving people the idea that he knew how to read, white man's leverage giving me the idea that I knew free

WHICH CROSSES YOU, WHICH COVERS YOU

Starting to go-to-law—to solve this union between truth and fact, for its passive dysfunction there is no variable but   lunge (the distorted pact among eyes and says) something humid about (us, driving) a Volvo (wagon) is the nostalgia that envy is   for air   (hollow building, brisk passerby, anybody breath, ex-breath, less even, can't distinguish fatigue from wanting   back   from never having)   owned (any), fashion (machines or masculine solutions for maladapted movement in thinking) Since when is dissent so reasonable, an orthodox eccentricity   how yours irritates me, but to radiance   I cannot say, but I do   like you   The truth is, fast sin, but I cannot say *fascination* when I mean hunting but I do   the truth is: I've indentured a future wherein this one I own now is humid and wanted then—the way I go to you

(went) Starting to-go-to-you- to-law-to-you to go law to you, starting to-go-to-law, you/law/you lost   me   too starting to notice

A Series of Events Linked by Casualty

Some public things   are so steeped in an imagined privacy that we keep forgetting to be, when trite is a
fitness   that stylized grief does not heal or resists healing, severenceless, maybe, but you are not alone ·
because you are not with me   I can't read the line on the subway graffiti   about 'you are the man you are
my other country' over and over without perceiving a belligerent ecstasy   I left my seat   like losing it   but
to be over-near-you   illusion of profit   the one who said

'We can fuck in the closet, that's my logic, but not every day, cause I'm workin' on my projects'   Next
thing you know   the way the sentence about shooting the elephant imitated the action of the gun   when
once you said   'come back' I could leave so satisfied having freedom with the option of covet, having
coveted freedom, having a covert need to be immature for you   the way you never knew you expected me
to: ambition   not-have-I-violated-the-times-for-chosen-offerings

So yes, somebody's death is the only physical way to say-so: yes   by September we had moved to
Hollywood and enrollment in anything was *happening*   so I'm dancing, like Russia of the USSR plus blood
of our own hungry angles as in Mr. Bo Jangles sinecured in Mississippi   Ask these bright men to get out of
our Chevy please, and put away their guns, we will hand it over peacefully   take your hand from over these
lips   violence is no longer (never) sexy, not that I have been violated for being chosen   Timber timberer
you go into yourself for the first time and are blind on a cold metal slide 4 AM   game of shoots and ladders
Teepee-ing the spook house   with a group of hypocrites like myself   to think that personality and behavior

are extricable or redeem one another mutually   This guilt makes us feel like a killer or a leader or mortal, together   My recognition that some people look like themselves cell cell, liver, mostly, comes early   at a time when I still doubt my own reflection   did it really happen that way   outside in a van, while the mother went in to grab a gallon of milk the father asked the child *should we leave her* meaning, run away with me forever, and the child said the no-syllable   romance I'm left with is this knack for the music of unconditional departures   harmless devastation like an unbodied swing which sways vacantly in a vacant park in Maine and in Harlem or when on Sunday when

    I was not her, you are not him

One Question Survey

Of the seize   on the invisibility of ease   on the reason reason

I'm looking at the castle   I'm foot back in the jungle   I'm well on my way   saying for impending glory .
they conceit before we can determine for ourselves what a way is and   what

wellness cash paid for,

and with cash pages the word
c a g e   became of the acre animal called   doll   mule   or this mule ain't from Moscow saying for
how come   Black people should practice horticulture   and so many hinges are lynchings (the word *because*
strings itself around my pelvis is my throat, because I said so, they both sway, they are both both) (how) to
say unique: New York, saying for your singular sacrifice (one) cannot name what's killing from what's offering
from what a killing to make a killing   saying for to have earned by gain, an assortment of cash product
until wealth   (sells itself)

Falsely urban or metropolitan (an ethic looking up at its fall), when conceived as a moment, is tempted
cheshire lips   tall building green tint to it (dissimulit of spring tree silver: fer) s p r i n t i n g, an affair, until
we're sprinting still Is this a corporation capital Or   am I in it

And yes it does feel like night habits and lunatics and shiny cars converge somewhere in your pucker I can hear my white shudder, shut off, harpoon, another lost equivalency, another miscellaneous hemisphere where still I am latch-afflicted, where still I want to be as shamble-beautiful as a late slashed animal, solving my mule dreams for when

ERRAND BOY FOR RHYTHM

With him the pinkest bracelets the photobucket the brand. Send man home man harp and chrome on the mantel on the wheel roll a tangible fleece notion of company in the background as we stand in the stomach of the room and Zydeco and unpatrol ourselves by the kind of oil that embellishes into stroll.

You know how to run out loud how to not run out   An invention, the dour wire on them laps   We're on the way somewhere   capital imagined   to a hospice factory jordache of a place   Two backs in the picture, making map of looking

Then one disappears in the forward and we have become somebody—

Within the pressure of idiom clung shape of one more so what as you say them in relation to my intrusions, valiant, or drunk, with this tender parachute on your lips

GUMSHOE/ A SEAT NEXT TO THE CEILING

(Scene: *Singers start to sing and fall in love with themselves. Hungry loon watching the television program in the mirror as she combs her hair into an ideology of hive which utters barbed wire around the family and scam traditions like when everything was silver and green until somebody turned flesh. This record of somebody turning.*)

I got rubato and I got so jolly over…

But my good breeding came to my rescue and I answered Yessir

And I began humming snatches as a domestic animus begetting flesh and I began again yes-ing humming I'm-so-full, I-could-be-your-threshold

What globe was on my heart revolving, what billow was solved like ignition and cleanness, what joke is the one where you told yours yes until it separated as scissors hyperextended or the back of a fending hand, or the dandy vogueing hand, or the camera flanked and pendulum and mineral poisoned from under itself   and became this rebel, barrel, question

What globe left on my heart, dissolving as he gets on the telephone and says all his words for me are figments of radio over surfaces of vogue pray, or to abdicate my shape and become a reich, a limit, or say so We who are proximate, still not discrete, stop distance from counting as lend it the highest number:

texture texture structure isosceles,   Detective, there is nothing left to solve   You've been so prior, circle-skirts and parlors, merriment and sidewalks,

Walk skies. Let me climb let me climb let me climb,   (signed)   your Client, your Clementine

SPECTACULAR BROODING

Casual abandonments are noble I think

As I watch the mother finish leaving her child simply by being, daily

And so I break my habit, (stay)

Something kind and typical

Before a competent rebellion

Puts me in the Mind of

Ike's mood 50, six degrees of separation, you cry in your sleep how each world began differently   In mine
for example, two black men hugging, no chaperone, no domain to stone in them and it's patronizing that you
even like me again

Against your lazy sentences, about being about it—what brisk diplomacy—System—My Ships, have become
yours and reported and veteran, how distracted, how enormous, how tugboat, how come   High Risk

my sister, my sailor for instance   Centers in the circle of a crowd

MANY ALMANACS

Feeling situated and bait, I ask to play horseshoes, 40 feet from these digging sticks in either direction there is either of us reflected in the Milkman's greasy Raybans along with the glass jug of slim white liquid we are meant to drink and also to learn the difference between a staple and refreshment as it fits between intending and throwing it fits between closed eyes and blindness it draws a line timeless as wisdom and the come hither nomenclature, Sophia, phobia, be a man be a lady be somebody   We sense a planet courting a finish, some sheen, and we long to be the initials grafted onto the bottle dearly, or jar or rage or starlet or pharmacist, or certainly disarming   Sad turn sad turn sad turn   I skip it, to press my face against the fence and him   and this counts   in its inverse a tiny expanse of petunias and flutes reduces into how hot it is to be a kid to raise a kid to be a kid   to grow out of mittens and to throw out the bottom or leave it in the skip-turn or turn to it all southern climate, dismissive attentive and maritime

(AFTERWARD) NOTES ON A LETTER TO THE SINGER ABBEY LINCOLN FROM HER LOVER, ABRAHAM LINCOLN

I once received this astonishing letter, a truly atrocious one, especially upsetting because, just between us, most of what it said happened to be true. I sent it back. It came back to me. Sparring. The fix-blue mind could operate like a fugitive. Running from what. Running to something. Grace/the front row. And when you reach it. It doesn't exist.

I began praying in Paris. That I may not be a parody, that I may remain alert, naïve, piercing. I prayed from pairs of unreasonable meter, to where joy is sorrow unmasked. I prayed for at least ten years straight. Sometimes in public, when the brothels were full. Sometimes in Hollywood. Once upon a time they owned slaves/nowadays they rent them from the behavior of orators. I loved those men. It has nothing to do with Africa. Or a harp in the nightclub. Were you here to protect property like it was lives. Was I any of the difference? Fertile plots of storyland and rate times time spangled distance. Standards. Restrained urgency. When it finally cannot be judged it will be judged as jazz. You act like you know that insult by heart. But even that was a coincidence of the metaphysical world. It's cool, I'm black too. I can hear myself swallow into the microphone when he leaves in the middle of the show. As part of the song. Maybe we did what the music did, it's true. No truces. Locusts and doves,

You were a philosopher

You were a polygamous woman

You had the courage to defend yourself

It's always been like this

So if I had never met

anyone but you,

I would have known which way to go

AFTERWORD

For the first several years of my life I was pretty much locked in a house with my father who would sit at his piano all day and all night composing music, writing lyrics, singing. His work ethic was wild and disciplined at the same time and I just remember watching, having little interest in toys and games, just wanting to watch him work and being fascinated/transfixed. When he passed away my mom enrolled me in dance classes in hopes of providing me with a surrogate structure. I studied ballet, modern, jazz, and West African forms and I felt at home inside the strict training so I immersed myself as thoroughly as I could. The only element that really competed for my focus on dance and music (listening) was an interest in literature/writing. I had decadently monastic tendencies, and still do in these areas.

Negro League Baseball is my attempt to clear a field/invent a field/demolish and reassemble the field negro/house negro binary. The spectral shadow of my father is cast across the entire work, as its guiding ethic still places me with my chin in my hands crooking my neck to watch him work until he got so exhausted he would nod off, allowing me to rest my gaze. In the end, this could be seen as a typical case of girlchild neglected by her recklessly prolific father, but I remember communicating with him more than I do in my most verbal human relationships, voyeurism or not. As a result I think much of *Negro League Baseball* places me in the emancipated spectator role, and much of it is a new take on the blindfold test, me feeling my way around in the room of his legacy and its impact, trying to name the sights and sounds, trying to knock down a wall to make space for my own adjacent room and acoustic. It is reconciliation without reconciliation. I had to invent an impossible/mythorealistic place wherein he and I could have and insinuate the conversations he and I never got to finish in this realm, a place not too drastic, but not too casual either.

I'm afraid to evoke the word jazz which has become vapid and spangled through overuse and misuse (over-meaning), so I use the safest analog game, baseball (for nostalgia and to avoid nostalgia, for fun, for a false faith in tradition, to detract the fabulists), in hopes of conjuring the sense of isolated togetherness felt by me personally within the central relationship in the book, and by black people, especially black entertainers and artists, in any endeavor toward forms that do not wish to draw attention exclusively to race, but are forced to in a context where certain idioms of accepted and even encouraged rule-breaking are often seen as *scene*, or as some nuance of the dialectic between oppression and decadent experimentation. We need a place to play if we are going to have a game. (A context, surface and interior) (This is) Not so much a cry for re-segregation as a cry for omni-segregation, or the posing of the question what if for a time the whole league was the Negro League, and all the old rules fell prey to amnesia, so this was no longer so strange, all of us just being us.

—HARMONY HOLIDAY

Fence Books supports writers who might otherwise have difficulty being recognized because their work doesn't answer to either the mainstream or to recognizable modes of experimentation.

The Motherwell Prize is an annual series that offers publication of a first or second book of poems by a woman, as well as a five thousand dollar cash prize.

The Fence Modern Poets Series contest is open to poets of any gender and at any stage of career, and offers a one thousand dollar cash prize in addition to book publication.

For more information about either prize, or about *Fence*, a biannual literary journal, visit www.fenceportal.org.

FENCE BOOKS

THE MOTHERWELL PRIZE

Negro League Baseball	Harmony Holiday
living must bury	Josie Sigler
Aim Straight at the Fountain and Press Vaporize	Elizabeth Marie Young
Unspoiled Air	Kaisa Ullsvik Miller
The Cow	Ariana Reines
Practice, Restraint	Laura Sims
A Magic Book	Sasha Steensen
Sky Girl	Rosemary Griggs
The Real Moon of Poetry and Other Poems	Tina Brown Celona
Zirconia	Chelsey Minnis

FENCE MODERN POETS SERIES

Nick Demske	Nick Demske
Duties of An English Foreign Secretary	Macgregor Card
Star in the Eye	James Shea
Structure of the Embryonic Rat Brain	Christopher Janke
The Stupefying Flashbulbs	Daniel Brenner
Povel	Geraldine Kim
The Opening Question	Prageeta Sharma
Apprehend	Elizabeth Robinson
The Red Bird	Joyelle McSweeney

NATIONAL POETRY SERIES

The Network	Jena Osman
The Black Automaton	Douglas Kearney
Collapsible Poetics Theater	Rodrigo Toscano

POETRY

June	Daniel Brenner
English Fragments A Brief History of the Soul	Martin Corless-Smith

FICTION

ANTHOLOGIES & CRITICAL WORKS